Buddy Leads the Way

The story of a true firehouse dog

By
Frank P. Sullivan

Illustrations by
Teri Forero

Layout & perpress by: Y-NOT COLOR www.y-notcolor.com

In the late 1800's, on a cool spring morning, eight Dalmatian puppies were born on a horse farm in an empty stall. Dalmatian dogs were quite common in horse stables in those days.

It is said that George Washington's nephew brought the dogs from England to the American Colonies. Known then as coach dogs, they were to be used on his plantation in Virginia. Dalmatians are great companions for horses because they can run a long distance along side of the horse drawn coaches. They made excellent guard dogs when the horses and coaches were parked and unattended. They would keep the intruders away.

At the same time three baby horses were born. The dapple gray foals were of the Percheron breed who were bred for their strength and speed. When they were old and strong enough, their job was to pull heavy wagons and farm equipment. It wasn't long

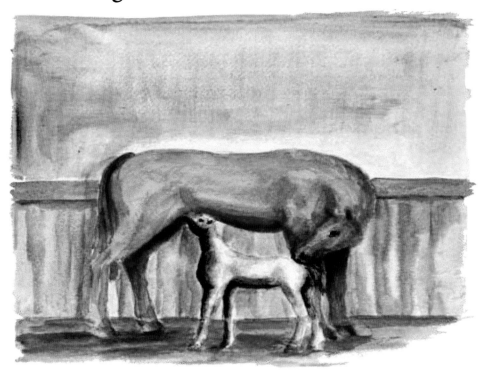

before the young horses were standing on their long wobbly legs. They began taking little steps to get close to their mother for warmth and feeding. They were named Jake, Rex and Joe.

As the newborn puppies started to grow, they began exploring their surroundings. They never wandered very far away from their mother except one particular pup named Buddy. Being very curious about the new foals Buddy would visit them often. Jake, Rex and Joe enjoyed playing with the little pup.

Soon Buddy began sleeping next to Jake at night. The three foals and Buddy became great friends. During the daytime, they ran and played in the fields. Although the horses were a lot bigger than Buddy, they were very careful not to step on him.

As the weeks and months passed, it was time for Jake, Rex and Joe to start their training as draft horses. They were going to be trained as a three-horse hitch. As the days of training continued, Buddy was right in the middle of them as if he was part of the team.

One day farmer Frank was having
trouble getting the horses to pull together.

Buddy sensed something was wrong so that
night Buddy unlatched the gates on Jake's
and Rex's stalls and made them switch stalls.

The next morning farmer Frank hitched up the horses the same way he did every day, but today, the 'Team' did great! Buddy knew Jake was the strongest of the three horses so he should be in the middle as the lead horse to keep the team working together.

Months passed and Jake, Rex and Joe were now strong, trained and ready for work. They would soon be leaving the farm and Buddy.

It wasn't long before two men from a nearby city fire department came to the

farm. They needed three strong horses to pull their new steam fire engine. When the firemen saw Jake, Rex and Joe, they knew right away they were the ones.

The beautifully matched team left the farm to perform this very important role in the fire department. After they left, Buddy became very lonely and sad. Buddy missed his friends very much.

A short time after Buddy's friends left the farm, farmer Frank received a message from the fire department saying they were having some problems with the new horses.

The next day the farmer loaded up his wagon for the trip to the city. Buddy sensed something was wrong with his friends and began barking and barking. Farmer Frank said, "Ok, Buddy, you can go, too."

Buddy jumped up into the wagon and off they went.

When Buddy and farmer Frank arrived at the fire station where Jake, Rex and Joe were stationed, it was a happy reunion for Buddy and his friends. "Wow! What a sight!" the Chief exclaimed, as he watched the friends greet each other.

Jake, Rex, Joe and Buddy sniffed and nuzzled each other until farmer Frank said

to Buddy, "Play time is over. Let's get to work and find out what the problem is."

The horses were hitched up to the steamer and off they went down through the city streets. Buddy was running alongside, barking all the way. When they trotted past the firehouse, the fire chief was pleasantly surprised at how well his horses were now doing. The team pulled perfectly.

The fire chief realized Buddy was the reason and asked farmer Frank if Buddy could stay with his friends and the fire department. Farmer Frank said, "Yes." He knew how happy Buddy would be to stay with his friends.

Now Buddy had a job to do and his natural instinct helped him do it well. He knew that firemen have a tough job fighting fires and saving lives so it was up to him to take care of the horses.

When the fire alarms would sound, the horses were released from their stalls. They

lined up in front of the steamer. The driver lowered the harnesses that were hanging above. You could see the excitement in their eyes. They were all ready to go. Once the fireman hooked up the Team, the station doors opened and off they went with Buddy leading the way.

As the steamer emerged from the fire house, black smoke was billowing from its

stack leaving a trail of smoke through the streets. The sound of the horses' hooves hitting the cobblestone street could be heard from blocks away.

In those days, big fires attracted crowds of people. The fire bells and Buddy's

barking would help clear the way through the crowded streets.

By the time they arrived at the fire, the steamer had a full head of steam and was ready to go to work! The steamer was hooked to the fire hydrant to pump water through the fire hose.

For their protection, the horses were unhitched from the steamer and led to a safe place. Most horses are afraid of smoke and fire. Buddy would stand guard to protect the horses from any harm and help keep them calm. Many times the firemen would cover the horses with tarps to protect them from sparks and embers from the fire and keep them warm on cold winter days and nights.

After the fire was out everyone returned to the firehouse where the firemen would clean and check their equipment to be ready for the next alarm. The horses were put in their stalls. They were cleaned, brushed and groomed. The firemen took a lot of pride in caring for their horses and loyal Dalmatian.

In those days, children and adults looked upon firemen with deep affection for their firefighting skills and the loving care they gave to their loyal fire house companions.

Buddy and his friends Jake, Rex and Joe answered hundreds of alarms over the years, until one day the city bought a new steam fire engine. This one was very different from the old one. It was motorized!

That meant they did not need horses to pull the engine anymore. What would happen to Jake, Rex and Joe? They were no longer needed.

This was a sad day for the firemen. They hated to see their trusty steeds replaced. They really loved their fire horses. For years of outstanding service, the fire chief decided he would send them back to the farm where they were born to live out their remaining years.

As a final farewell, the city hosted a parade and Jake, Rex and Joe pulled the steamer one last time through the city streets. The people lined both sides of the streets as they cheered and clapped.

But, what about Buddy?

Buddy was also very sad to see his very special friends go back home. He missed them a lot. Even though he occasionally responded to the fire alarms with the new steamer, it was no longer fun. Buddy spends most of his time watching over the fire station when the firemen are out on calls and keep the firemen company when they are in the station.

To make Buddy feel better, the firemen always kept fresh hay in Jake's old stall for Buddy to sleep on at night.

One day, firemen from Hose Company Number 5 came to visit and show off their new fire engine. Running along side the new motorized engine was another Dalmation named Missy. Buddy and Missy had never met before. They had been too busy doing their jobs with the horses at their firehouses.

Buddy and Missy ran all over the fire house getting into all kinds of mischief, knocking over water buckets, running in and out of the empty horse stalls. All the firemen enjoyed watching them having fun. Buddy and Missy became great friends and the firemen let them play together often.

As the days passed it became noticeable that Missy was going to give birth to puppies. On a cool spring morning in an empty horse stall eight new Dalmatian puppies were born to Missy and Buddy. As Missy was caring for her puppies, Buddy stood by proudly looking down at the new generation of firehouse dogs.

As the days and weeks passed, Buddy and Missy's pups became old enough to leave the fire station. The firemen kept one puppy and named him Rex. Missy returned to her fire station where the firemen were anxiously awaiting her return. Even with little Rex around, Buddy still missed his old friends Jake, Rex and Joe. He always slept in Jake's stall. The fireman continued to keep fresh hay in the old stall knowing he missed his friends.

In spite of everything the firemen could tell that Buddy's heart was not in the job like it used to be. Now that little Rex was able to fill his father's place the firemen knew what they had to do.

One day the fire chief asked Buddy if he would like to go back to the farm to be with his friends. Buddy barked and barked and jumped up and down. "I guess that means yes," said the fire chief.

The next morning the fire chief arrived at the fire station to pick up Buddy. Sitting in the chief's buggy was Missy. She will also be going to the horse farm with Buddy.

As they drove away Buddy gave a few good barks as if to say good bye to the firemen and especially little Rex who would stay and carry on the traditions of the fire house dog.

Buddy and Missy lived happily ever after
with their best friends, Jake, Rex and Joe.

The End

Of This Adventure

About the Author
Frank P. Sullivan

I have been a member of the fire service for over 45 years both as a volunteer and as a paid professional. I retired as a Captain from the Miramar Fire Rescue Department, Miramar, FL. During these years, I have owned Dalmatian dogs who are also known as fire house dogs and were mascots in the fire department. The Dalmatians were considered as family members and they performed two functions:

They helped in teaching small children fire safety in the public schools and also visited children's hospitals and nursing homes where the Dalmatians are always a big hit!

When the Dalmatians and I are out during public functions, I am always asked the same question, "how did the Dalmatian become part of the fire service?"

"Buddy Leads The Way" tells the story.

Frank P. Sullivan with his Buddy

Made in the USA
Charleston, SC
20 September 2013